Maria

A Story of Mental Illness and Healing through Faith and Spirituality

MARIA LORETTO

ISBN 978-1-63844-393-3 (paperback)
ISBN 978-1-63844-394-0 (digital)

Christian Faith Publishing, Inc.
832 Park Avenue
Meadville, PA 16335
www.christianfaithpublishing.com

Printed in the United States of America

To my children
My sun, my moon, my star

To my family

To Carlos

Chapter 1

THE BEGINNING

I was born on March 21, 1972, in Schenectady, New York. My mother tells the story of the day when she went to an old castle-like historic hospital in Niskayuna county, knee-deep in snow. My father was working on his doctorate degree in economics at Rensselaer Polytechnic Institute. My mother worked full-time at home, taking care of my two older sisters, ages three and one-and-a-half: my dearest Isabella and Gabriella. My mother would take us to a small playground in the courtyard of their apartment building. People wondered how my parents managed being student parents of three under three. My mom also tells the story of when the doctor asked what her husband did for a living, and when she responded, "He's a student," the doctor replied, "Perhaps you should think about birth control." My mom was brought up old-school by my devout Catholic grandmother whom we called Mimi. Being the oldest of nine in a strict Catholic household, I suppose this was the first time my mother was presented with the idea of birth control. But she agreed, and the story went on. Luckily my paternal grandmother, Tita, had come to visit my parents from their home country of Nicaragua to help.

As the story went, my father was at RPI on a full scholarship, but when I was six months old, he was summoned back to Nicaragua to comply with work-related commitments. He could not finish his doctorate degree, but he went back home to a great job and a comfortable life. They built a house in front of my Tita and Tito's home (my paternal grandfather whom I look a lot like). He was a musician and songwriter in Nicaragua. He wrote some of the most beloved Nicaraguan folk classics. He sang of the beauty of Nicaragua and of its people. I shared a strong bond with him, even though he died shortly after I was born. He was artistic and compassionate, a spiritual dreamer, and we were connected. At least that was my fantasy.

I lived in Nicaragua for the first seven years of my life. Memories are vague: playing with paper boats in the rain with my sisters and cousins and making mud pies along the side of the house with my sister, Gabby. Some memories are not so vague as when my mother abruptly yanked my pacifier out of my mouth and threw it into the woods behind the house. I remember when my favorite little glass broke—my *gordito*, which I used to drink milk out of every day. I was a sensitive child, needless to say.

On my seventh birthday, my mother threw a beautiful party for me. She was a master host. She dressed my sisters and I in beautiful white dresses. My dear aunt, Coco, walked into the party with what I thought was the most magical pink dress, and it was for me to wear. I felt beautiful and special. I caught a glimpse of myself in the mirror though, and I noticed a little blemish beside my lip. I stared at it intently and just as quickly fixated on it. I could not stop thinking about how *yucky and gross* it looked. Suddenly I became melancholy, self-conscious, sad, and withdrawn. But at picture time, I faked a smile and thought about the blemish. Years later, I found that picture in my mom's house. It was framed along with my sisters' in their white dresses. I looked at the blemish and at the sadness in my eyes.

Another one of my vivid memories was a day at the beach with friends and family. I was still in a dreamlike state, as most kids are at that age, when in the distance, I heard a boy calling out to me, "Loretto! Loretto! What an ugly name! It sounds like a boy's name! Hahaha!" His laughter echoed in my mind, and it woke me up. I was paralyzed, mortified, and ashamed in that moment. Perhaps most kids would have shrugged it off or retorted with a clever comeback. But to a tender heart like mine, it was an imprint. The internal struggle, conflict, and battle with my name began but more so with my identity.

Around that time, my mother was pregnant with my youngest sister, Bella. Due to the political unrest in Nicaragua, my mother went to Louisiana to stay with my father's aunt who lived in a beautiful, old-style New Orleans home. We went to school there for some months while we awaited Bella's birth. One of the first days of school, I remember eating my bologna sandwich when a boy spilled milk on my skirt. It seemed as if the whole cafeteria laughed at me. I was embarrassed and wanted to hide. So I did, metaphorically.

When my sisters and I got home from school that day, we saw our mother come around the corner in the hallway. *Oh my goodness!* I thought. The baby was born. We cheered and screamed with excitement and laughter. We ran to the crib to look at her. She slept peacefully on her belly with her little butt perked up. I could not contain my excitement and disbelief. My baby sister was small, precious, and dressed in white. The room was cold, and the shades were drawn. The moment was pure, and I heard my heart beat.

We returned to Nicaragua for a brief period as the Sandinista revolution got underway. Things in Nicaragua were unsafe as a war brewed within. Military tanks patrolled the streets, and gunshots were heard in the distance. Many family members took refuge in our house. They slept wherever there was room. There were mattresses against the windows to protect us from flying bullets. One dark early morning, I was awakened by my parents and was told to get up quietly and to follow them outside without a sound. Outside was a car from the American embassy that would transport us to the airport. We were fleeing the country with the clothes on our backs and $2,000 in my father's pocket. The day became excruciatingly hot as we waited on the floor of a cargo plane with other Americans who were going home. My mother was an American citizen (her father was American), so she was able to seek refuge at the embassy and arranged for us to be placed on that cargo plane. I remember feeling hungry that day. Someone gave me a bite size chocolate for the ride. This memory was anything but vague.

Chapter 2

WELCOME TO AMERICA

We arrived in San Antonio, Texas, at my grandaunt Mercedes's house. I stood outside her front yard and noticed how green the trees were, how warm the breeze was, and how crisp the leaves sounded. There was a table in that front yard where my sisters and I would sit with an ESL teacher who taught us English. On the side of the house was a one-bedroom in-law apartment where we would stay until my father found a job, and we could rent a house of our own. My sisters and I walked into the apartment and felt an eerie sensation. Isabella, my oldest sister, vomited shortly after walking through the apartment, and we teased her that the house was haunted. My parents, of course, brought a priest to bless the house with holy water.

The next few years in San Antonio were quiet, blissful, and innocent. We were placed in a humble Catholic school that we loved. My father secured a job at the university teaching economics and was able to finish his thesis and doctorate. My mother was our school's secretary and liked being close to the nuns and to us. My first day in second grade began with my teacher asking me what my name was to which I answered softly, "Loretto." I did not speak English, and my pronunciation of *Loretto* in Spanish sounded foreign to her. She asked me to repeat it, yet she could not understand me. The other students sat silently and watched the exchange. In the face of embarrassment, it quickly occurred to me to tell her that my name was Maria (my first name). She understood that, and I exhaled. For the next five years I would be called Maria at school and Loretto at home. My identity conflict grew, as did my struggle with self-acceptance and, more importantly, with self-love.

Hidden behind these blissful years was the darkness though. It took the form of self-loathing to a point that I could not look in a mirror or at a picture of myself without wanting to cover my face figuratively. I was ashamed of who I was. I looked within, and all I saw was insecurity and self-doubt. I told a friend in fifth grade that if I could change anything about myself, it would be my nose. My nose. As it grew, so did my obsession with it. Body dysmorphic disorder (I later learned) had reared its ugly face.

My parents rented a house, and we moved many times while they saved money to buy a house of their own, which they did when I was in seventh grade. That year, we were also told that our beloved school was closing, and that, I would be going to a new school for eighth grade. I was enrolled in another Catholic school which was not as humble. It was located in a very traditional upscale part of town. You could see the difference in the cars people drove and the airs people had. I was sick with anxiety as my first day approached. My uniform had not arrived yet, so I had to wear regular clothes on the first day. As if being the new kid wasn't enough, I stuck out among the students because I, unlike the others, was not in uniform. I was nervous that first day. When the teacher called out our names, I heard, "Maria," and I reluctantly responded. My sister and I had had a conversation the day before that this would be a good time to go by a more American mainstream name. We both agreed Maria was too ethnic. As the teenagers we were—we just wanted to fit in. I went straight to the teacher the next morning and told her I did not get a chance to tell her that at home, I go by my middle name, Loretto, and *Lorie* for short. And so I became Lorie all through eighth grade and high school. This was a new identity, a new name, and a fresh start. My essence kept getting lost and buried.

The cool girls befriended me, and I was glad to have been welcomed. Yet the feeling of being the new kid never quite went away. And I never felt connected to anyone. I looked at the less-than-cool girls, and I thought, *I'm not what I seem.* I never wanted anyone to think I was more than what I was—human. I played basketball, which was my saving grace. But something happened that year when I switched schools. I began to feel mute, hidden, invisible, and lost. And it only intensified when I entered high school.

High school was not unlike many teenagers' experience. I was wrought with insecurity and a longing to fit in. But for me, I believe there was an unidentified low-grade depression underneath the mask. I felt like a small fish in a deep sea of two thousand students. I did not feel like other typical American kids because of my Hispanic background, which most kids did not understand or appreciate. I was still going by Lorie, which hid my true identity and made me feel even more invisible and fragmented. There were some incidents when kids teased me about my big nose, which made me want to crawl deeper into my skin. A boy in my government class said my nose looked like a ski slope. A friend once made a reference to how big my nose was compared to her tiny one. My boyfriend was told that if he and I had kids, their noses would be huge. I laughed it off, and my heart sank into deeper waters.

When I was sixteen years old, my family and I moved to Bogota, Colombia, due to a job offer my father received. It was a drastic change in culture and a confirmation that I did not belong. I attended an American school which was mostly made up of well-to-do privileged Colombians and expats. I gravitated towards the few American out-casts and fit in perfectly there. Our time in Colombia was short-lived as we moved back to Texas only six months later. I was excited to be back in the United States and at my old school. But that was short-lived too. At the end of my junior year, my parents announced that we were moving yet again and, this time, to New York. My parents found a house in Connecticut, and I attended Greenwich High School for my senior year. I knew no one, and these were the people with whom I would graduate high school. Again I gravitated toward the outcasts: long-haired musicians who wore heavy metal T-shirts and smoked weed. I was intimidated by the popular clicks and wondered why I couldn't be in them. I guess that just wasn't in the cards for me.

Around this time, I distinctly remember sitting in my room having my first thoughts of suicide. I longed for professional help—

someone who could help me understand myself. But I guess I did not speak loud enough of my intentions because my dark side, too, was well hidden. I was a master at pretending everything was fine because there was a side to me that could be very silly and funny. I could laugh incessantly with my sisters and friends. In fact, there was a side to me that thought everything *was* truly perfect, and I could feel quite elated some days. The dichotomy was a conundrum to me. I had learned early in my life to pretend and portray that everything was fine and perfect—slap a smile on your face and hide any feeling that was not a happy one. This can be quite damaging for someone like me who was adept at hiding. But I was a pro and an actress at heart.

I will always thank God that in that high school, I was exposed to an array of elective classes from which I could choose. I wound up in a psychology class, and I was smitten from day one. Where school had never been a strong suit for me, I found the subject matter in this class riveting and stimulating. I was amazed that I could actually dedicate myself to the study of emotions, the psyche, and to the understanding of human behavior, perhaps maybe my own? At that moment, I knew what I wanted to do. I was starting to actually get interested in the idea of college and visited a few in the area. I fell in love with Sacred Heart University which was close by. The campus was beautiful, and the people were welcoming. My mother and I met with an advisor, and I felt that, that was the right place for me. Perhaps I had finally found a fit, dare say a home.

But the dream was short-lived. I was crushed to find that my parents were moving back to Nicaragua after eleven years in America. This meant that I had to move back to Texas to live with my sisters who were at the University of Texas at Austin. I was thrown into a larger sea of people, as the university was made up of more than fifty thousand students. To make matters worse, my parents informed me that we would spend that summer in Nicaragua, which was the last place I wanted to go to. I felt I had no ties to Nicaragua, and that, going back there was irrelevant to me. I remember my mother's last words before the trip though. "You'll see, you'll fall in love there."

No way, I thought. *I'm going to marry an American.*

Chapter 3

CAN YOU GO HOME AGAIN?

My mother was right, as she often is. Sure enough, at one of the many parties and celebrations I attended that summer, I literally saw Diego across the room, much like in a movie. He was golden. It caught my attention that he was talking to my cousin, which meant I had a way in. His fair hair glistened. He was tall and lean, his face perfect, his eyes sparkly. He had an elusive quality about him. He looked distinguished and as if he came from old money. He had impeccable manners and crisp clothes. He was cool, and I was not. He was out of my league.

A love affair began that summer that was like no other I had ever known. I idealized him, idolized him, and wanted to be just like him. My insecurities climbed to new heights, feeling unworthy and as if I was not good enough. I tried to do everything I could to deserve being with him. He was very appearance-oriented, and it triggered that side of me that also demanded self-perfection. My weight went up and down, more down than up. I went to drastic measures of dieting to stay thin. I focused obsessively on my hair, makeup, and clothes, and of course on my nose. Never had I wanted a nose job more than at that time. I figured if I just fixed my big nose everything would be *perfect*. *I* would be perfect. I tried obsessively to be perfect and everything he wanted me to be. The distorted insecurities and obsessions were draining and completely oblivious to me. I was just not good enough.

I majored in psychology at the university, becoming more and more passionate about my field. I was excited about my classes and felt elated learning about topics that were fascinating to me, like the human condition. This was a taste of my true self which of course at some level, I was trying to find. But it was impossible to be objective about my own ailments and to diagnose myself. I was too close to it. My feelings could not have been more foreign than what I was learning. But schoolwork and studying—I could control.

The next four years of college, being Diego's girlfriend (as was my identity then) were some of the darkest yet polarizing moments of my life thus far. Never had I loved a man so much yet felt a deep, dark hole inside. It was a contradiction in terms of which I could not make sense. I adored him; I worshiped him; I couldn't wait to see him every weekend; yet inside, I felt an abyss of melancholy. It is clear to me now that at that stage of my life, my depression had worsened unbeknownst to me. I studied about mental health every day, yet I could not identify my own symptoms. The insecurity and self-deprecation I experienced were not typical teenage angst, and I needed help. Only God knows why I did not seek professional help. I truly thought all my ailments were due to my own shortcomings, or maybe, I just didn't know myself.

I made it through college somehow and graduated—one of the proudest moments of my life. I did get nose surgery during that time as well. I went to a butcher in my country that ruined my nose, and after the surgery, my nose looked deformed and mangled. Waking up from the surgery and looking at my profile in the mirror was traumatic. It could not get worse at that point because the obsession became relentless. I learned to live with it somehow, and life went on.

Diego and I were both living in Nicaragua at that time, starting our careers. We had been dating for four years then, and we were at an impasse. Neither one of us knew with certainty where the relationship was headed or which way we wanted to go. But I knew it was time to define it because I knew we could not date indefinitely. Neither one of us was sure if we wanted to get married, but we had a conversation at a pizza place one night, mostly me telling him that we had to decide where we were going. Deep down I told myself,

What are you saying? You don't even know what you want. If I had had the words back then, I would have said, "I'm not sure what we should do at this point. I am not sure if I want to get married, and I don't think you know either, but I also know it has been a long time, and I don't think we can continue indefinitely." Oh, how clear hindsight is. That night, nothing was resolved, and dinner went on. As we talked and reminisced about old times, I mentioned to him, "You know, you've never brought me a serenade." He chuckled, and I thought, *How I would love that.*

A few months later, we were engaged. I was getting ready to go out with him one night when I heard beautiful acoustic guitar strings playing outside. I chuckled to myself, *He is bringing me a serenade because I told him that the other night.* When I opened the door, he had a two-dozen bouquet of red roses in his hands and a smile on his face. He did not have to say a word. *Oh my goodness*, I thought. I was in shock. I couldn't believe what was happening. My feet left the ground, and I began floating. It was a surreal moment. So many things were racing through my mind. After the beautiful music ended, we sat down on the couch and began thinking about and planning the wedding. We were elated and a little shocked. Never had anything felt so right—almost.

The next few months were a fairy-tale. My parents were in good financial standing. My father was secretary of foreign aid in the government, and buzz was in the air. *Wedding of the year*, I was told, were among the whispers. Nothing but the best. The party would be memorable. Three hundred guests were invited, ranging from the president's daughter and her vice-president husband to ambassadors to old friends and family. It was a whirlwind. I was caught up in the excitement of wedding bliss. Nothing short of a Gatsby novel were among the fantasies in my head. My mother and father were taking care of everything, so I could just enjoy and say "yes" or "no" to every detail. My dress was of fine silk—the softest material I had ever felt. My oldest sister wrote me a poem inspired by that same silk and gave it to me on my special day. Among some of the most lavish gifts I received such as a car (from my parents) and a honeymoon cruise from Diego's cousin, this poem was the most valuable gift. It was simply titled "Bride." Throughout that time, I wanted to make sure that I was not just getting lost in a Cinderella movie. I would turn inward periodically to check how I really felt. I was happy. And like I told my sister, "There is nothing telling me no."

I wondered how I was going to feel the day after the wedding though. I was afraid of waking up only to regret it. But I didn't. I woke up, and I was happy. I was surprised that I felt peaceful. It felt natural. Every time I looked at him, I thought, "I love this man." That feeling was never in question.

Subtleties crept up immediately though. On our honeymoon, I remember feeling a bit awkward yet excited about our life together. It was a contradiction beyond comprehension, despite my psychology training. When we returned home, I felt elated that I was married. At work, I beamed and gushed giggling with coworkers. Yet every afternoon, when I got home from work, I would curl up in a ball in my bed and checked out. Diego noticed there was something wrong.

Around that time, I also auditioned for a play at the American embassy. I felt the need to connect with my true self and with my soul of an actress. My love of acting began in fifth grade. After which, I continued classes throughout high school and college almost majoring in theater. Deep down, I truly believed I could and would be an actress if it was possible. I already was one inside. Diego came from a much more conservative background where acting was considered liberal and low-class. Clearly he did not approve of my acting classes in college and certainly not of auditioning for a part in this play. To make matters worse, the rehearsals were two times a week and in the evening. In Diego's conservative mind, the fact that his new wife was not going to be home two nights a week for dinner because she was acting in some show was unacceptable, and he was not pleased throughout the entire length of rehearsals. Reluctantly he attended the play on opening night, and I dare say he quite enjoyed watching me onstage. It was just the beginning of a long battle to be understood and accepted by him and to make him see me. The inner struggle to be authentic and have him love me for it was torture. Perhaps the conflict was in my mind, but I truly felt that he wanted me to be a certain way, to fill a certain role that was in his mind, not mine.

I felt invisible in my own home and alone in a marriage. It was not much different than how I felt as a child. As I processed in therapy many years later, I felt like an ornament for the better part of my life—something sparkly to look at but a lifeless object people use to decorate *their* tree.

But during that first year, something happened that changed my life. Pope John Paul II was coming to visit Nicaragua, and Diego insisted that we go, much to my reluctance. My faith was lukewarm at that time, and I would have much rather stayed at home than to be in the hot sun with masses of people for hours. We had the privilege to sit at the very front, in comfortable chairs, and I liked dressing up. Little did I know what was about to happen. I saw the Pope arrive, and my heart started beating fast. I looked behind me and saw a sea of humble, poor people filled with faith and joy. That image was also an imprint and resembled a letter I had written to my Tita when I was twelve years old in which I wrote about wanting to help the poor in Nicaragua. I thought to myself, *I have to do something to serve.* The next day, Diego and I went to church and joined a catechism group. We began a yearlong journey of faith and service. My spiritual journey had begun, albeit short-lived.

Our first year of marriage came and went. Diego focused on preparing for the GMAT and completing applications to top MBA programs in the United States, thankfully, he received an acceptance call from Northwestern University in Illinois, thirty miles or so north of Chicago. I was elated. It was unreal to me that we would be moving back to the US and would be going back to school. Not only was I thrilled for his acceptance, but of course, I was also looking forward to applying to graduate school myself. I could not get out of Nicaragua fast enough. I loved Nicaragua, but I had not really grown up there, and living there was a bit of a challenge. In addition, the fact that I had unfinished business academically made me want to go back to the US even more.

Chapter 4

THE DESERT

It was an ecstatic time for both us. We were overjoyed with anticipation for what the future had in store for us. We closed shop in Nicaragua, sold or gave away most of our things, and boarded a plane to Chicago. I felt like a brightly lit Christmas tree, instead of an ornament. On the plane ride, we planned how we wanted to decorate the apartment and our lives. I distinctly recall the day we arrived in Evanston. I must have been floating on air that day because I felt two feet off the ground. The colors seemed so vivid and bright, the leaves crisp, and the air clean. When I look back now, I can clearly see the few minutes of mania I felt upon landing, only to crawl back into my quiet hole as the days progressed. Nights were sleepless and days overwhelming. My feelings were a kaleidoscope, ranging from joy to mania to fear to sadness. Most people would say that what I felt was normal given the circumstances, but staying up one night crying for eight hours paralyzed with anxiety did not feel normal.

Things settled down though when we found an apartment and classes began. I got a job working at the university and immediately began applying to graduate school. It was very difficult for me to go to school and work full-time, so I started taking classes part-time. It was challenging, but I pushed myself to the limit and somehow accomplished what I had set out to do. Diego was focused on school and fighting his own demons. It was an extremely competitive environment that slowly picked at his self-confidence. It was hard to see him struggle with self-doubt, always wanting the best for him. Not only did I quietly long for him to achieve his material goals, but more importantly, I wished for peace in his heart. I always wished he saw himself through my eyes.

Around this time, I decided to see a plastic surgeon in Chicago and consulted him about correcting my nose. It had been mangled for five years, and I had always had a deep, black hole in my heart because I hated how I looked. I had nose surgery that year, and the doctor's work was flawless. My nose was perfect and looked natural. When he took the bandage off and I caught a glimpse of my new nose, I couldn't focus because I was afraid of finding fault with it. But as I honed in, I felt pretty and happy, perhaps for the first time. I looked forward to getting ready every day and actually looked forward to being around people. In other words, I somewhat liked my appearance and did not want to hide, almost.

The closer I looked in the mirror, the more I scrutinized over little hairline veins that were apparent as a result of the surgery. This caused my nose to get very red very easily. I would do incessant mirror checks to see how my nose looked and obsessed over photos to see how red my nose looked. All I could think of was Rudolph and shuttered. A few months later, at my daily routine of scrutinizing, I remember thinking, *If the doctor had just nipped it a little bit more, it would truly be perfect. Eh, maybe I'll get that done in the future.* A disorder I knew nothing about but had started in fifth grade was now rampant—body dysmorphic disorder, I would later learn.

When Diego graduated from his MBA, he received a job offer in Sao Paulo, Brazil. I also received an acceptance letter from Northwestern as a full-time graduate student. I held the letter in my hand, thinking how much I wanted to stay in Evanston to finish my program. I had waited so long for him to finish school, in the hopes that I could then go to school full-time myself. But that would not be the case. We were going to move to South America. I contemplated the idea of staying behind to finish school, but I just could not do it. So I put my plans on hold, packed up, and moved. I left the US with a heavy heart. But part of me was also excited about the new adventure. We bought some books and tapes and began learning Portuguese. "Your life is like a movie," a friend said.

Chapter 5

BRAZIL

The move to Brazil was nothing short of adventurous. I felt so safe and secure with Diego by my side. He seemed to always be in control, and he was a pillar of strength. He delved into his new job courageously, and I began my life in Sao Paulo shopping at the corner street market. We stayed at a flat for a couple of months while we looked for an apartment. After looking at sixty or so apartments, we chose the second one we had seen. It was located in a lovely, upscale, desirable neighborhood. I felt so lucky and blessed. I had a charmed life. We wined and dined with the expat community from all over the world in the best restaurants in Sao Paulo. We traveled throughout Brazil and South America with my husband's banker colleagues and their spouses.

The first six months was a time for settling in. I reveled in decorating the apartment and making it cozy. It was a nice break for me after working full-time and going to school. The homemaker fantasy ended though, and I began to feel restless, bored, and lost. I didn't have a work visa, but I know now that if I had wanted to, I could have looked for opportunities to be sponsored by a company in order to work. But the more time I spent at home, the lazier I got, and my mind wandered. I slept the day away and began a vicious cycle of binge eating followed by restriction and obsessive exercising. Obsession also manifested in ritualistic trips to church every morning at 7:00 a.m. I could hear the church bells from my bedroom window early in the morning, and they were calling out to me specifically. I took the short walk to church every morning, with my heart beating quickly, and attended mass dutifully. Something was happening, but I was oblivious to it.

One of my lazy afternoons in the apartment, I was watching CNN, and I saw an interview with a famous medium that was talking about communicating with spirits. I almost had an out-of-body experience watching this because I felt like the messages were aimed directly at me. I felt as if God or the universe was communicating with me through that precise show at that exact moment. I was overcome with an eerie sense of faith and a realization that life after death truly did exist because now, I had proof. I called Diego immediately and told him about the show, and he thought the topic was interesting.

So I continued going to church every morning and began reading the Bible obsessively. I was overcome with a feeling that God was calling me to serve him and to spread his Word. I felt I had a divine purpose in life, and I was finally getting in touch with it because God himself was with me. I distinctly remember that during this time, I felt a heightened sense of awareness and alertness. I felt awake. I felt full of nervous energy and as if I had a mission to fulfill. I remember thinking that this is how priests and nuns must feel when they are called to serve the church and join the clergy. I even questioned whether I was being called to leave Diego to join the church or whether I had missed my calling. At that point, I started believing that no exchange with anyone was random, and that, I had to spread God's Word to every person that crossed my path. And that was precisely what I did. In every conversation I had with anyone, I intentionally made sure to talk about God and faith, in hopes to inspire others to seek God as well. I distinctly remember a phone conversation with my sister during this time in which she said to me, "Hold on a minute. Slow down. I don't quite understand what you mean. You're talking too fast.'"

I had a journal for years, and one of those nights, I remember feeling particularly inspired to write. As I began pouring my heart out, I remember I couldn't type fast enough. The words, thoughts, and ideas were coming so fast that my hands could not keep up. I wrote a random mix of memories, thoughts, ideas, and prayers. At one point, I began to free-associate and wrote word after word with no rhyme or reason. I cried; I shook; and I trembled because I was overcome with an acute intensity of feelings. It was a long night, and as the sun came up, I heard Diego open the door of the room. He stood in silence looking at me—his face pale with concern and worry. It was 7:00 a.m. I had been writing for ten hours straight. He asked, "What are you doing?" By the look on his face, it dawned on me that it may be a bit odd for him to find me still writing from the night before. I felt compelled to cover it up and explain that everything was okay, that I had gotten inspired the night before, but that, it had been very therapeutic for me. He looked at me skeptically but said, "Okay, get some sleep." When he walked out the door, I took a shower and began my new life. I felt as if I had been cleansed and renewed. I felt a few feet off the ground again. I immediately went to church, and I recall that my senses were heightened. I felt on edge, extremely alert, and uncharacteristically energetic. I was very awake but in a dreamlike state and didn't sleep for days.

The second night, I went into the room and began writing again. As the night progressed, I felt myself getting farther away from my body. I started writing and drawing sketches and graphs of ideas that could not come fast enough. I laid out papers on the floor with books and quotes from the bible. In my mind, so many things were becoming clear. I could see my life mapped out clearly before me. In that moment, I felt I was healing many wounds. I pulled out a book of poems written by my great grandmother, as well as a book written about my grandfather. I felt his presence palpably in the room with me. I truly felt he was there with me in spirit, speaking to me through my soul. My thinking became delusional believing I was channeling spirits of famous figures such as Princess Diana, the Pope, and the president of my country. I genuinely believed I had messages I had to convey to them and plotted how I was going to do it. I honestly felt that the Holy Spirit was entering my body and cleansing me. It was a night of madness. God was there, but the evil insanity was too.

Due to this newfound awareness and cleansing, I firmly believed I was ready to have a child. I felt I had reconciled with my demons, that I was in a better place and ready to bring a child into the world. After months of trying to get pregnant, though, I visited a gynecologist who recommended fertility treatments. I began taking medications, and shortly thereafter, hormone injections daily that would increase my chances of ovulating and fertilizing. It turned out I had polycystic ovarian disease. At that time, my sister-in-law in Costa Rica was also trying to get pregnant, and we were both experimenting with the same treatments. She recommended I have surgery on my ovaries to cauterize the cysts. I flew to Miami to have the surgery, which was very successful. Following the surgery, I began ovulating regularly, yet I was still unable to get pregnant. I was not aware at that time how the hormone injections were altering my mood and emotional stability, which was compromised to begin with. The madness had become an uncontrollable tornado.

I clearly remember sitting at the kitchen table one morning, ruminating as usual. I had so much idle time on my hands that I spent the entire day in the apartment floating around in a numb-like state. My mind was slowly drifting and getting more and more tangled in a web of insanity and distortions. That day, I decided my new focus was going to be my appearance. Since my nose was perfect now, and I spent hours at the gym to lose weight, all that was left was my hair and a tan. I had spent several years without my usual highlights, and my hair was a bit dark, although in certain angles, it looked chestnut. I had spent so many years with a mangled nose job, feeling ugly and hidden, that now I wanted to shine and have fun. I wanted to look my best. So I got up from the kitchen table, got on my bike, and impulsively rode to the nearby salon to get my hair done and buy some tanning sessions. I figured that with highlights, being thin, and having a perfect nose and a tan, I would look and feel perfect—an elusive pursuit masking a search for inner peace. I was not quite sure what I was trying to accomplish, but the rush and energy was too hard to contain. I was so lost in my fantasy that I could not objectively reflect that the only makeover I needed was on the inside.

So I rode my bicycle down the street when suddenly, I felt overwhelmed and wrought with anxiety. I questioned if this was silly, crazy, and clearly impulsive. My heart raced and something deep inside me told me to stop and go back home. *Don't do this*, was all I heard in my mind. My body shook, and it was difficult for me to focus. But I pushed on despite that internal voice and made it to the salon. I lay on the tanning bed as the fluorescent lights turned on. I situated myself, and I was given a towel to cover my face. I held it in my hand for a split, decisive second, but I thought, *I might as well get some color on my face as well.* And I put the towel down. In a matter of seconds, I could feel my face stinging. It was as if needles were piercing through my face. Thank God in that moment I thought to myself, *This doesn't feel right*, and I grabbed the towel and covered my face.

After the tanning session, I looked in the mirror, and to my horror, I noticed that the cartilage around the tip of my nose had gotten burned on the inside, causing a protrusion on the outside. It is hard to explain the damage that had occurred, but it was as if you could see an imperfection on one side and a bump on the other, which made it look like I had two tips. In addition, my nose then looked abnormally pointy, and the horror I felt was still indescribable. *This cannot be happening*, I thought. The anxiety I felt as I rode back to the apartment was traumatic, as I have no recollection of it. I paced in the apartment the rest of the day, checking my nose incessantly in the mirror to see if it had gone back to normal. I ran desperately to the pharmacy to buy burn cream. I lay on the couch, cried hysterically, rubbed the cream on my nose, and bargained with God. Diego came home late that night, and as he walked in the door, I ran to him crying, saying, "Look! Look at my nose! I ruined it!" God bless that man's soul because he kept looking at me and said, "It looks fine. I don't see anything." Inside I thanked him for that. But I knew it was not true. No matter how many times you tell someone with body dysmorphic disorder that they look fine, they will never believe your lie. And you will always know you are a freak.

From that point, I don't quite remember the sequence of events as I again fell into a depressed state and obsessively ruminated over my nose. When we were in social settings, the anxiety was debilitating. My face would flush with no explanation when I was around people. I was consumed with violent obsessions. *Everyone is looking at my nose* was the only thought that occupied my mind.

Diego and I went to a picturesque town nearby one weekend to sightsee. We came across an artist who wanted to draw a caricature of us. My heart raced, and my legs grew weak. *Oh my goodness*, I thought. Reluctantly I posed with Diego as my vision became blurry. The one and only thought that ran through my mind during the entire drawing was my nose and how this man was going to draw it. Naturally when I looked at the picture, my heart sank. He drew my nose abnormally thin and pointy.

Later that week, I was in my bedroom one morning staring at the drawing and developed a form of tunnel-vision fixation on my nose. I was paralyzed with anxiety. My heart raced. I felt weak; and I started to cry. I knew something was wrong. I called Diego, and I said to him, "Diego, I have to go see a doctor. This is not okay." I called a clinic to make an appointment with a psychologist, but they said they only worked with psychiatrists on staff. I said, "That is fine." And so began my wavering relationship with medication.

When I sat down with the doctor, I began telling him about my nose. He not only said I was a perfectionist but diagnosed me with what was called dysmorphophobia (now known as body dysmorphic disorder). He was so quick and certain about my diagnosis that I almost felt a relief that there was a method to my madness, and it had a name. He went on to explain the disorder and also diagnosed me with major depressive disorder. My mind quickly went to the episode of my sleepless nights, writing frenetically. But I glossed over it and told him that had been more of a spiritual awakening. He prescribed Zoloft, and I promptly went to the pharmacy. I took it as soon as I got home and waited.

I experienced some side effects for the first few days, such as headaches and diarrhea. But one morning, I woke up and realized that my first thought had not been my nose. I forgot about it for one brief moment and felt a glimmer of hope.

Chapter 6

THE WINDY CITY

Diego and I unexpectedly learned that his job was relocating us back to Chicago. I was in shock and disbelief, in a good way. I was finally going back to the graduate program I had left behind and to which I had so desperately longed to return. I could not start packing fast enough. Diego's job made the move seamless, taking care of all the details. Packers came to the house and meticulously counted and packed every fork and spoon. The rest was a whirlwind I don't quite remember, but before I knew it, I was strolling down the streets of beautiful downtown Chicago. It was summer, so the sun was shining, the breeze was warm, the lake was bright, and the trees vibrant. We settled into a temporary apartment for a month until we found a beautiful two-bedroom apartment in that same area, overlooking Navy Pier and Lake Michigan. I was in awe of my good fortune and of how blessed I had always been. I thanked God for every minute. And I thanked Diego in silence who was making all this possible.

I distinctly remember driving on "Lake Shore Drive" toward Northwestern. I knocked on my supervisor's door who was delighted to see me and to learn I would be back in the program. Everything felt right with the world. I began classes that fall and reveled in the work. There had never been a better fit for me since I had walked down the halls of my humble elementary school. I walked through the bookstore skimming textbooks for graduate school, and I could hear music in the background of my life. *Blissful* cannot begin to describe what that time felt like. I searched my soul to connect with the deepest part of who I was. Finally, the inside was matching the outside in regard to achieving my goals and expressing who I was. I reconnected with my true self through the rock music I loved so much in my teens. I went to record stores and bought old albums I used to own, like Led Zeppelin, Aerosmith, and of course, Guns N' Roses.

But reconnecting with my longtime obsession with Axl Rose went beyond the usual admiration. My mental health conditions always had to take it to the next level. My delusions took me to obsessive, delusional thoughts that I was destined to meet him, that we would have a relationship, and that I was meant to be with him. Now I know it sounds like a bout of delayed adolescence when most teenagers fantasize about their favorite actor or musician. The difference with me was that I was absolutely convinced that this was going to happen. I believed I was very close to these delusions becoming a reality. I then understood that my longing for being loved for who I was, was what I was really fantasizing about. I longed for being loved not for what I appeared nor for what I reflected to the other person about themselves nor for what the other person wanted me to be but just loved and seen for who I was—strengths and weaknesses. Deep down, I believed it was what we all want: to feel that somebody loves us, just the way we are. I also then understood that unconditional love has to start with ourselves. But in order to love yourself, you have to experience unconditional love first. I later found that unconditional love which saved my life.

At the end of my first year of graduate school, I learned I was pregnant. It was a fantastic feeling. After three years of undergoing hellish anguish from fertility treatments, the pregnancy test yielded positive. How could I be so blessed? How could I be so lucky? I ran to the doctor's office to confirm the pregnancy through a blood test. I began my ultrasounds, and our families were overjoyed. It had been a long journey for all of us. They, too, had been waiting anxiously for that little miracle to come. One Friday afternoon, I went to the six-week checkup. The technician was doing the sonogram as I watched the blurry shapes and sounds on the monitor. The technician looked at me and said, "There's no heartbeat." Whatever anyone could imagine that I must have felt pales in comparison. I was numb. I walked home that afternoon distraught at the thought of telling Diego. It was a somber night. The D&C could not be scheduled until the following Monday, so we spent the weekend in a stupor, knowing there was a being in my belly that had no life. Monday morning, the D&C was done, and I felt the sounds and suction. I thought, *This is the procedure that is done during an abortion*. I thought of someone I knew, and I prayed.

It would be another year before I learned I was pregnant again. This time I was cautious, almost expecting the worst. But as the weeks went by, the pregnancy seemed to be moving along famously. I was jubilant and blissful. My life really was a fairy-tale. When I graduated with my master's degree, I was four months pregnant. I look at the pictures now and can't believe my first baby was there with me in this special moment, enmeshed with my body and soul. I thought of the countless moms, single or not, that face difficulty balancing work and child-rearing. And I offered prayers of gratitude.

I accepted an offer at a mental health agency working as a psychotherapist. *What would I do when my baby was born?* I thought. But I began my job and thrived in my new role. I worked hard to learn and grow professionally as my belly grew alongside it. I felt beautiful and ethereal. What would I do when the baby was born?

It was around this time that I went to a Guns N' Roses concert in Chicago with a friend. Coincidently that night, Diego would be away traveling for work. I fantasized that the fact that Diego was away was a sign that I would meet Axl Rose that night. Somewhere in my mind, I honestly believed this to be true, and that, I would go with him to his next destination and never come back. Whereas for others this might be nothing but a fleeting fantasy or thought, I actually thought this might happen that night. After the concert, my friend and I tried to go backstage, but of course, this did not happen. So I drove my friend forty minutes back to Chicago.

After I dropped her off, my adrenaline began pumping. I could continue the five minutes home or—? So I turned the car around and drove forty minutes back again to the venue. I parked in the back parking lot, in front of the tour buses. I saw people going in and out of the back door. Everyone had a backstage pass hanging from their necks. I looked in my glove compartment and saw my old badge from work. Perhaps if I hung it from my neck, I could casually walk in. My heart raced as I plotted this scheme. I truly thought I would walk in and casually introduce myself to this musician, and the rest would be history. We would talk all night and fall in love. What was wrong with this picture? I sat in my car over an hour debating whether or not I should risk attempt going in. Suddenly, a lady with a clipboard and badge approached me and asked what I was doing there. Like a fool, I asked if the band was still around. Clearly they were not, and I felt idiotic. I turned the car around in embarrassment and drove home.

This was only a sign of things to come. That manic, out-of-touch-with-reality part of myself was on the horizon. The same part of me that would later cause dire circumstances in my life and in the life of those I loved.

The day finally came when I experienced the most defining moment of my life. In a few pushes, my first baby, Fernando, came into this world at 8:03 a.m., weighing eight pounds and eleven ounces—"a big baby," the nurses repeated. My mom was by my side, and Diego at the other. They watched Fernando peek his little head out at his father and grandmother. When I met and held him in my arms, I felt peace and time stood still. I looked at his face and thought, *I know you.*

The next few days and weeks as a first-time mom were dizzying. I felt disoriented most of the time. My sister, Isabella's, support was unconditional, as she had, had her firstborn son a couple of months prior. The first trips to the doctor were chaotic and almost comical but in a dark way. Diego and I scrambled, unsure of what we were doing. My mother worked tirelessly to help us. My father also traveled to Chicago to meet his grandson.

I did not know it at that time, but my mental illness subtly but fiercely manifested itself. It crept up like a snake that blindsided me, yet came in for the sting with a vengeance. This time, it came in the form of a relentless obsession with my son's sleeping schedules.

I watched the clock all day to make sure I was putting him down at precisely specific times according to his pediatrician's book. I blocked out the light in his room during sleeping. I turned on white-noise machines and tiptoed around the room. I became infuriated with anyone who was being loud or not. It was maddening for me and for those around me. My husband commented I was being too extreme and rigid, but no one could get through to me. I would let Fernando cry, so he would learn how to soothe himself and go back to sleep on his own. I would put headphones so as not to hear him or the knots in my stomach. Not a moment goes by when I think of this that I don't feel those knots of regret. I could never allow myself to contemplate what he may have felt. Mere thoughts of that pain me still. I make a concerted effort not to go there in my mind. I know all moms have their haunting memories of guilt. And we are not alone.

Time passed in a stupor, and before we knew it, Fernando was seven months old, and a sibling was on the way. I could not wait for him to have a brother or sister. Unfortunately, that pregnancy did not come to fruition. It was a tough miscarriage but very different than my first loss. Time continued at lighting speed though. Fernando turned one year old, and again, we discovered that another sibling was growing in my belly—this time, healthily. The pregnancy went famously, and Juan Pedro was born on July 29, 2005. Juan Pedro was a special boy. His skin looked and felt like silk, and he glowed like an angel. His thin, fine hair was mousy brown. He was alert, active, and had a twinkle in his eye that shined day and night. Fernando would kiss his brother's forehead and would lie down next to him. Of course, this only lasted until Juan Pedro could move around and take Fernando's toys. Then the usual brotherly fighting began, which triggered insanity for me. I had my hands full with two boys now. It was not easy, and it was not glamorous. I was blessed that I could choose to stay home with the boys and even had a babysitter to help out. But I did not realize how privileged I was. I just wanted sleep, silence, calm, and normalcy, whatever that was.

Gradually I began to feel that I somewhat had the hang of having two kids twenty-one months apart. I developed a routine, and luckily for Juan Pedro, I did not sleep train him. I cradled him to sleep every night, yet his sleeping never lasted long. Juan Pedro was not a good sleeper. He woke up at all hours of the day and night and would stay awake for at least an hour, if not more during the darkest hours. As a toddler, the moon mesmerized him. Excitedly he would look at the night sky and say, "Look at the moon, Mommy!" And I kept this in my heart.

But the lack of sleep was torture for me. It was slowly chipping away at my fragile state. Unbeknownst to me, my depression began again. I felt lifeless most of the time. I watched the clock incessantly waiting for the boys' nap times, so I could sleep. But sometimes, it was only ten minutes when their naps overlapped. My body, mind, and soul shut down. It is astounding to me now that at that moment, I was unaware of how blessed I was. I had two beautiful, healthy boys. I had a good man by my side that worshiped his boys. I had a lovely home, financial stability, help, family, and abounding love. But that is how depression is. It is cruel, indiscriminate, and its darkness overpowers particularly dim light.

Chapter 7

THE BIG APPLE

When Juan Pedro was two months old, my husband came home one night to tell me that we would be relocating to New York. His voice faded as he started telling me the details, and all I could feel was a literal ache in my heart. I felt stunned, speechless, and crushed at the thought of moving—again. I felt a nauseating hole in my stomach. I deeply felt something bad was coming. *More darkness lay ahead*, I thought. Call it woman's intuition or mother's instinct, but I somehow knew this was not good news. And I worried for our future.

Naturally I went into robotic mode—packing, planning, selling our home, and looking for homes in the New York area. The last few days seemed almost too much to bear. The absurdity and chaos in my psyche worsened. The anxiety brewed like a volcano on the brink of eruption. We arrived in New York City one rainy afternoon to a beautiful apartment on the East Side. The bank Diego worked for arranged for us to stay for two months in a spacious two-bedroom, two-bath apartment, just steps from West End Park. The following day, I woke up to pouring rain. Diego left early for work, and I found myself sitting on the windowsill staring at nothing, and I cried. But when you have kids, time does not stop long enough to wallow. I went to the grocery store with my two babies. We could barely fit down the narrow New York aisles with a big stroller and a baby carriage. The rain came down hard. That afternoon, I did not know what I would do or how I would make it through. Next door to our building was a bookstore where I would hide. Fernando left my side for one second, but it felt like a lifetime. I could not find him. I panicked, and for those two minutes, I lost my mind. This was too much.

We began looking for apartments in the city and for houses in the suburbs. We were scattered and lost, literally. My sister, Gabby, who lived in the city was an invaluable support system. She found a babysitter for me, held my hand, and walked me through the abyss. Sometimes she would take care of the kids herself, so Diego and I could house hunt. It was around November that I went to the doctor for a checkup. Of course, I was pregnant again. What had I done? I sobbed at the doctor's office wondering if I would miscarriage again, which my body, mind, and spirit could not handle. That night, Diego sat quietly, contemplating, each of us alone in our thoughts. But we carried on.

We found a house in Connecticut in December, but it would not be available until March. We had to leave the New York apartment, so we packed up and went to another temporary apartment in Stamford, Connecticut, until the house was ready. One late, dark evening on January 1, Diego began unloading the boxes from the U-Haul truck under a snowstorm. I watched him through the window as I held our baby, and I thought, *What a strong man made of steel.* I, on the other hand, was barely able to put the kids to bed without crying. Again I found myself in unfamiliar territory. Diego left for work early the next morning, and there I went venturing out in a new town looking for the pediatrician's office in complete disarray.

It was during this time that a lady from our home country came to live and work with us. It was a blessing I did not realize I needed at that time. As always, my sister-in-law had looked out for us as she encouraged this nanny to come live with us and help us take care of what would be three kids under three. And that was exactly what she did. Her help was immeasurable and unquantifiable. She helped with very tough work, mostly holding me up.

On March 1, we moved into our new home on another snowy day. My belly grew, and in a stupor, we tackled the sea of boxes. We began putting things away one by one. I began searching for a preschool for my beautiful firstborn who was growing into a precious toddler. His hair was golden, and I started calling him my *sol*, my sunshine. Juan Pedro was not far behind. He was a fast crawler and a joyful boy. His rich brown eyes shimmered and twinkled, and his smile got me through the days. I protected him at all times from his older brother who was not happy about sharing his toys. I would ask Fernando, "Who's my sun?" And he would jump up and say, "Meeee!" Then I would say to Juan Pedro, "Who's my moon?" and he would raise his hand eagerly and responded, "Meee!" And my baby girl grew inside me, ready to join the family, another angel in my path. My star on the horizon.

Summer arrived, and so did Maria, my third and last child. My star was born. She was a porcelain doll with an ethereal beauty of unexpected proportions. She resembled my maternal grandmother, Mimi. I considered my grandmother's name, Leonie, for her especially because her zodiac sign was Leo. Then I considered naming her Mimi, like my grandma's nickname. To this day, my daughter, Maria, tells me she would have liked to be called Mimi. It made sense because she will always be connected to her great grandmother.

That November, Diego went on a business trip to South America. I distinctly remember sitting at the computer late one night in the family room. Everyone was sleeping, and the silence was deafening. I began crying and sobbing. I was losing my mind. For months, perhaps years, I had been floating around in a dense, hazy fog. It baffles me now to think of how I got to the preschool and back those days. A lot of those memories are buried in my body, mind, heart, and soul because I was too numb to store them in consciousness. I was absent, away in a very dark place. But I had reached my limit. I called Diego overseas and told him I was not well. He told me he would take the next plane home and flew all night. I counted the hours, minutes, and seconds until he got home. I paced around the dark, quiet house. At dawn, he walked through the door and knelt beside me at the desk where I had cried for eight hours. Quivering I said, "Take me to the hospital." And I fell into his arms.

We arrived at the ER, and I was quickly admitted to the psychiatric unit. Diego had to leave, and the staff walked me to my room.

It was a stark, stale room, and a Jamaican woman with big eyes lay on the bed next to mine and stared at me blankly. I curled up on my bed and wept in this nightmare where I paradoxically felt safe. I knew this was where I needed to be. I went very far away in my mind and rested.

The next day, the daily routine of group therapy sessions began, as well as medical checkups, meals, art, pet therapy, and so on. I distinctly remember a flower arranging class which for some reason, I connected with. I was put on a regimen of medications, and I painfully missed my kids. My family was sideswiped. Diego was broken.

Two days after arriving at the hospital, I was transferred and transported to a nearby psychiatric hospital, and I settled into my new quarters. I had a meeting with the psychiatrists and clinicians, and I was diagnosed with bipolar disorder. Suddenly everything made sense to me. I had spent years trying to figure myself out, and in a matter of seconds, my life flashed before me, but now with some sense of an explanation and more importantly, an understanding. Every moment, every incident, every significant emotional experience and episode made more sense. Memories of my moodiness as a child, the dark nights when I would lay awake for hours crying, scared, and holding a rosary made more sense to me. The impulsive, risky behavior in high school followed by bouts of suicidal ideation was something I could now begin to understand. I understood that the episode I had in Brazil was my first manic episode, and that, it was not properly treated. All the fertility treatments had altered my hormones which compounded my mood cycles intensely. The following five years of being pregnant and having babies and miscarriages coupled with a cross-country move were more than my body and mind could take. And now, after years of keeping the pieces together in order to survive and fulfill a role, I broke.

So this was the beginning of a long and arduous recovery process in which I will always be. You see, with bipolar disorder, you are never cured or out of the woods. You live one day at a time, and you work at staying stable by following certain recommendations such as balance in sleep, meds, psychotherapy, a support system, etc. And it is precisely when you feel you are out of the woods when you need to be the most cautious.

To me, it is analogous to walking a tightrope. Every day, I grab my pole and put my feet on the rope, without a safety net as it feels like sometimes. I take every step slowly, carefully, and calmly, and try to keep my balance. Sometimes I sway to the right, sometimes to the left, but my focus must remain on regaining my center, on taking another step, and not falling. It requires concentration, mindfulness, and some taming of the beast within my mind. Of course, every day, I live with the fear of falling off that tightrope. Sometimes it gets awfully shaky, and I struggle not to fall. And sometimes I realize that the fear of falling is worse than the fall itself. Yet it is only in facing the fear head-on that you break from its hold and make it to the other side—the next day. And if you do fall, it is into your safety net; those who love you—your angels, God, a higher power, meditation, friends, therapists/doctors, your church, your family, a stranger— and you can let yourself weep knowing you are safe. Some people never realize they have a safety net, which is why I am writing.

Chapter 8

THE MAN WHO WOULD CHANGE MY LIFE

When I returned from the hospital, I was in a haze for about six months, which turned into years. I barely remember driving the kids to and from school. Such a simple task, yet so daunting and overwhelming for someone in my state. I now look back and cannot imagine what I must have seemed like to people around me. My eyes were vacant, my skin pale, a ghost. The memory of missing my son's little Mother's Day celebration at preschool haunts me. I know mothers can relate to the guilt we carry, like of these moments. But I have to let go and forgive myself—for that and for so many things.

Two years passed in a debilitating depression albeit with medication. I knew I had to function but could only do so if I disconnected from everything entirely. I was detached from everyone and everything, practically lifeless. The boys fought incessantly. I almost had to dissociate in order to tolerate the screaming and their fights. It was too much to bear. My heart could barely tolerate it. Every day ran into the next. I shuddered when I awoke to the thought of another one.

The nanny's help, to this day, remains the saving grace that got me through those years. And my husband, my dear husband, who worked tirelessly to provide not only financial stability but more importantly love, safety, and a pillar of strength on which to lean on. He was not only a provider; he was a father.

I began looking at elementary schools for the kids. In a fog, I walked into a school which name I do not remember and was following along in a tour. And there he was—the man who would change my life. He introduced himself, put his hand on his chest, and said his name which I did not hear. To me, he was just another nameless, faceless person in the distant fog that was my life. He spoke to me about the school, but I might as well have been looking at bare walls because I was not there. I sat at a kids' table when suddenly, he knelt beside the little chair in which I was sitting. And just like that, I woke up. I could see his lips moving, but I could not hear a word he was saying. I stared intently into his eyes, and my face lit up. I smiled and fell into a tunnel to his soul and my own. I felt awake, alive, and I giggled for the first time in many years. I simply felt. I felt I had known him all my life. I felt comfortable talking to him. He made me smile and laugh. It was infectious. And I couldn't get enough.

I could not wait to go to the next activity at that school. I tried to look pretty, put on makeup, and washed my hair for the first time it felt like in years. I had not looked at myself in the mirror in years despite the obsessive mirror checking. I had not seen my soul since those elementary school days at my humble Catholic school. And there he was. And I, just like an adolescent, stood still waiting for him to notice me. He came toward me, and again, he talked, but I could not hear his voice. I wanted him to notice me, to like me, to see me. And sure enough, he did. "You look pretty," he said. You look pretty—that would sustain me. I was emotionally thirsty and spiritually starving, and I gorged those words. As I walked away, he gave me his phone number and told me to call him if I had any questions about the meeting or the recommendations. *I think he may like me*, I thought. I hoped. But he was hard to read and too charming. That weekend, I thought of the man the entire time. And I felt pretty.

The following Monday, I was shopping for a dress to wear to an event I would attend the following week with my husband. It was ten in the morning. I walked aimlessly in the shopping center. Then my phone rang. I knew it was the man who would change my life. I looked at my phone and saw his name. *Here we go*, I thought. There was no turning back if I answered. And without hesitation, I smiled and picked up the phone. I took a deep breath, "Hello?" I said. I knew deep down that I could not let this go. The stakes were high. But I did not waiver. I knew.

He came to the mall for coffee, and we sat and talked. This time, I *could* hear his voice. My hands shook, and I was embarrassed because of it. I was nervous, and it showed. This time, I could hear the words coming out of my mouth, but I was not sure what I was saying. I explained my mental health condition to him—why? I was not sure. I just knew him. I felt I could tell him anything. We finished our coffee, said goodbye, and that night, I sent him a text. "Thank you for the coffee," was all I wrote. And he knew.

What came next was a whirlwind of madness that would last three months. It was a frenzy of emotions and frenetic energy. And the man came along for the ride unknowingly. The roller coaster came to a halt though when I could not sustain the internal chaos anymore. The pressure broke me, so I told my dear husband. Our relationship crashed, and our marriage died that very moment. The following months were filled with such pain and heartbreak that I am incapable of revisiting with this pen. But I do know that it quickly reached a point of no return. I fell apart. My life as I knew it slipped out of my hands. It is scary to even revisit now because I ended up in the hospital again where time stood still for one week. I could not gasp for air during this most desperate week of my life. What was happening? Where was I? Certainly not oriented or steady. When I was discharged from the hospital, my dear husband asked for a divorce. And so it began. Part of me felt relief that the roller coaster came to a stop. The metal bars lifted, and I got off. My husband was so brave to take that final step. Always strong and courageous, I thanked him in my heart because I was too weak to do it.

The next few months are hard to revisit. I look back now, and the best way to describe it is that each day, I crawled through clouds and fog without knowing what I would see or find if I ever got to clarity. My feet were not firmly on the tightrope; in fact, I was hanging from it with one arm and swaying. All I could see was the darkness that lay below. I was no longer numb. I was scared. I had been in the worst manic state I will ever experience. What was apparently the lowest time in my life felt more like euphoria and frenzy. And I honestly thought at that time that was the best I had felt in twenty years, juxtaposed by the fact that I was at the psychiatric hospital with others like me. The priest from the church came to see me. My mother was in a trance—much like my own. And all I obsessed about was him—the man who had changed my life. I was like a caged lion, taming myself in order to get out of there. The seconds, minutes, hours, and days of waiting to see him were painful. I stared at the clocks, at the sky, and the moon in angst waiting to see him again. I frantically called him every chance I got. "Please come get me," was my plea. He did not. He, unlike me, had his feet on the ground. Meanwhile my parents and sisters were living this torment with me. They were steadfast and carried me and carried on. How? I will never know. And then, there was my husband, my dear husband—the man of steel, who was keeping it all together for the kids and their stability. Where was I?

I left the hospital, but the horror continued because I was flying high. My father stayed with me while my family continued on with their daily lives. In addition to the medication I was put on, I self-medicated with food and cigarettes, gaining weight every day. I stuffed down every bite, along with my anxiety, in order to calm down. My compulsive rituals controlled me, and I lit a cigarette every twenty minutes. Ironically, I was able to attend my therapy sessions three times a week and played the sanity card at which I was so adept after years of practice. I manically called and texted him to schedule our routine frenzied meetings. He was still on the roller coaster with me, blindfolded. And I was addicted to the rush.

The divorce proceedings continued, and the sky grew darker. I do not think I can accurately capture through written word the despair I felt about the divorce. It is impossible to attempt to explain why I wish it on no one. Those who have lived it simply understand.

The clouds started to lift ever so slightly when I found a place for me to live with my children. I desperately longed to create a home for us, as well as a new beginning. The delicate balance between excitement and mania blurred as I decorated my new home. The days passed in a hurry, yet I could not go fast enough. A new chapter of my life had begun. I was living on my own for the first time, and I was under nobody's thumb. But the growing pains began as well. I was an immature child, buying anything I wanted with no regard for cost or how it would be paid. I incurred debt shamelessly with the ten or more credit cards I foolishly obtained. Our first Christmas that December dawned a tree that overflowed with gifts as well as anxiety. My house looked like a winter wonderland, a good friend said. But that was all it was—a fantasy. My family came to visit that Christmas and huddled around me as they always do. We did a gift exchange, and my heart beat rapidly as they opened their expensive gifts that I could not afford. I knew they were concerned. They looked at me and felt my mania lurking.

My father stood by me steadfastly. We sat at the kitchen table one night making a budget that did not cover my expenses. "I will send you money every month," he said. "You will need it." And he was right. He did not realize at that moment that his financial and emotional support would be embedded in my heart. I would not realize it either until much later. And he will never know to the extent that he held me up, like the pillar that he is.

Chapter 9

YEARS OF MADNESS

The new year arrived, and it was time to hit the pavement. I spent my days searching for work and searching for my new identity. Contrary to how daunting unemployment can be, I felt exhilarated. I could not buy and shop fast enough to make my life perfect. All the things I had not done, bought, thought, and expressed were coming with fierce speed that I could not keep up. There were not enough hours in the day or credit cards available to keep up with me. Then I got the call. I was offered a job interview at an agency for which I did not remember applying. I did not even know what agency it was, and naturally, I was shocked to even be called. I barely remember the interview, but I do remember the salary which for all-intensive purposes was very good for my profession but modest for what I truly needed to support myself responsibly. Regardless, the offer might as well have been a million dollars because I had never made my own money. So to me, one self-earned dollar was a dollar more than I ever had.

I was thrilled, ecstatic, and very scared. I arrived the first day with my foggy glasses and floated through it in slow motion. And I continued floating through the following days, months, and years at that job. I appeared, put together and masterfully learned my tasks, but I was desperately keeping my illness hidden and protected myself from being exposed. I was mentally ill but skillfully performed my job like a thespian in character. I rushed out during lunch hours to meet with the man, as well as before and after work. Somehow I juggled the chaos that had become my life: job, the man, my children, money, my condition—all very grown-up challenges I was not ready for. I was a fragile child, sick and lost. Yet my illness tricked me into thinking this was the best time of my life. Perhaps it was in certain respects. The constant contradiction of euphoria and darkness depleted my essence. I walked the tightrope every day, but it became exhausting year after year. I gorged food continually and smoked compulsively to "survive." I was blind to my own demons that cleverly tricked me like the magicians they are. I was a puppet doing the dance of freedom.

The years morphed, and the beast within silently maimed me. The debts and the panic grew silently. All the while, the act continued. But my performance was losing stamina. The mistakes were evident, and I could not mask them as adroitly as before. I was an actress at curtain call performing her last show, after which I collapsed and confessed to my family and to him that I was in trouble. They rushed to my rescue. The little bird that had tried to fly had fallen and injured itself. Time to nurse it back to health.

So again, my sisters and he bailed me out. But time was running out too. The final curtain dropped. and I lost my job. I had no choice but to take my mask off. The show was over, and I stood backstage with no costume under which to hide for the first time in my life. The growth spurt was fast and sudden. Just when I thought the darkness had passed, the black sky closed with a fury, and the thunder began. The worst of storms was coming, and this was not a play. The safety net under my tightrope was gone. The stakes were too high because the wager was my life, plus I had three children to think about. I sunk into the deepest layers of depression but now without foggy glasses to blame. I could see everything, which was terrifying. I slept the days away, barely capable of completing daily tasks. *But I cannot go back there*, I thought. "The hospital is not an option," said the man who had changed my life. I had fallen to my knees on the tightrope and was not sure if I could get back up—worse, if I wanted to get up. Why not let go?

In my mind, I always had the image of a candle, and to me, its flame represented my level of hope. Sometimes the flame was bright, and it lit up an entire room. Its warm reflection was so bright that you would think the flame could easily start a fire if not careful. Other times, it was dim and flickering, with a blue hue at the bottom. Yet the fact that it was still burning meant I was still in the fight hanging on. Sometimes the candle was on, but you could barely see the flame. Its flame was so dim that you'd forget it was on until you'd find it the next morning, relieved it *didn't* start a fire. Hope became an important word for me. I knew that if I ever lost the yearning to make a difference, to connect, and to inspire, I would be in trouble. I knew that if that flame went out completely, I was capable of jumping off that tightrope because without hope, I feared I had nothing. There had been times when the candle was out, but a long wick was left over that could still be reignited. But if I ever got to a point where the wick ran out and the candle could no longer be lit, that's when I would make arrangements and organize my things to drop the pole and let myself fall. And that's where I was at this point in my life. I sat at my kitchen table in the dark. I dotted my Is and crossed my T's. I ran down the calendar—when would it be? But my kids! My kids! They were the last strand holding me on the rope. And at that moment, without faith, I reached for my Bible.

The days passed, and my sister, Isabella, came out to the rope on a harness and carried me. The rest of my safety net watched intently and prayed. The fury of desperation set in. I could not tolerate my inauthenticity anymore. I had to trust, as fearful as that was. I had to trust God because there *was* no other option. "Staying on my knees or letting go was *not* an option." I heard a soft voice in the distant— my sister, Gabriella—whispered, "C'mon sis, *you can do this*!" She had no fear in her voice or doubt in her mind, never flinching nor wavering. Her rational voice told me I *could* get up. For someone whose feet live firmly on the ground, she believed. She dreamed with me. She actually thought I could. So I believed too.

I opened my private psychotherapy practice a month later and got myself back on consistent treatment. I rented an office five minutes from my house. I made it beautiful and made my performance a reality. With such calm fury, I began my life without masks or costumes. This time, I was playing myself. My caseload grew and came together steadfastly. And as usual, I was still seeking. It is time for the next act. God knows I cannot stay stagnant. But at least now, I am getting closer to my truth. The tightrope is firm, the walk steady. I have a harness, but I still have to walk it every day. My safety net is there, and I am not afraid to fall into it. I know I am safe, and I can climb back up. I will always be scared; I will always be cautious; but I will always go on—carefully. And I will never stop learning, pondering, hoping, and dreaming. I am better but never out of the woods. Just learning, every day. What now? The journey continues and like the man who changed my life said, "Life goes on."

Chapter 10

COMING HOME

In the fall of 2019, I started going to a new church. My kids started a new school, and I agreed to take them to the Sunday teen mass at the insistence of their dad. Little did I know what was about to happen for the second time in my life.

At mass that day, I felt my heart overcome by the beautiful music. I gazed in awe at the altar and at the images of Christ. My heart beat fast, and I looked around me. I was mesmerized again and scared.

In the days that followed, I felt a pull to go back to that church. I went to mass again the following Sunday, and I could not contain the emotions that were overflowing within me. I tried to resist, but a few tears were impossible to hold back. My heart beat a little faster, and I soaked in the power of God's energy.

I attended a gathering the following week and met some people from the parish, as well some priests. I spoke of how I wanted to get involved in the community and how much I connected with the church services. I felt a bit disoriented, and I couldn't help but wonder, "Was another episode coming on? Was I losing grip?" A quiet fear had started, but it became loud enough to keep me up at night, often in tears.

For twenty years, I had been spiritually paralyzed and petrified of getting close to God again. I had discounted my first spiritual awakening in Brazil because it was intertwined with my first manic episode. Back then, I had not been able to tease out where God began and my madness ended. So I shut it all down.

Reluctantly I called the church and made an appointment with a priest, looking more for guidance and therapy than anything else. I sat in the confessional with Father David's sweet gaze on me as he provided support and reassurance. He assured me that God's voice was nothing to fear. He provided concrete and logical guidance on how to proceed. He recommended I seek guidance from a spiritual director as I embarked on this journey of discernment and ponder. As he spoke, I looked intently at his facial expressions for cues as to whether or not he thought I was crazy. As I spoke, I did the same and monitored myself. I attended a one-day Marian retreat that weekend which confirmed for me that I wasn't. I felt at peace at the church. My heart sang, and it felt right to be there. I looked at other people around me to reassure myself that this was normal. Twenty years ago, during that manic night with my computer and my diagrams, the Holy Spirit had come and gone, or so I thought. Now I realize that what I had done was closed the door on my soul and on my true self. What had started and stopped in one night twenty years ago was now reawakened. And I am not afraid this time.

Last week, I met with the director of theology at a nearby university. He was well trained in the area of psychology as well as religion. I could tell by his questioning and by my story that he was gauging my mental status. I told him I was taking my medications, attending therapy, sleeping well, going to work, and taking care of my kids. To my relief, he said that by adhering to treatment, my functioning seemed typical, and that, he was not concerned about this being a manic episode yet. He paired me with a spiritual director with whom I would start my journey.

This is a very scary time for me. I am overwhelmed with deep and intense emotion. But at the same time, the puzzle pieces of my life are starting to corner up, and I can see bits of the picture. I know I have always been a child of God, but now, it has transitioned from a theoretical knowledge to a palpable reality. I know now in a very authentic way that my identity is intrinsically tied to serving God. I could always envision my life helping and inspiring others by sharing my story and tying mental health with spirituality, yet one big piece was missing: actually feeling God's presence in my life in a tangible way.

My journey has truly taken a right turn, and I am ready to walk the tightrope firmly, with God securely as my safety net. My love affair with God has been rekindled, and I am overjoyed. I am realizing I am most happy in his orbit, and that, that is where I get energy, air, and life. It is where I belong. And this is not a manic episode.

A few weeks ago, I dreamed I was standing in line on a sidewalk with a group of people. I looked toward some bushes, and I saw a little boy dressed in white motioning to something or someone. As I reached those bushes, I saw a man barefoot in a puddle of water turn toward me. It was Saint Pope John Paul II. I reached my hands up toward him, and he poured the cleanest, glistening water on them. The stream of water continued cleansing me as he spoke to me in Polish. I woke up with tears of gratitude in my eyes, and every night, I pray to God to be visited again.

Sure enough, in a more recent dream, I was looking at a medal of Mary whose shine and sparkle was brighter than the sun. The medal was attached to a chain filled with so many large diamonds whose shine and brightness were blinding. I followed the chain of diamonds and found my own mother holding the other end of it. This sentiment I dedicate to all the mothers reading this and relating to this story of hope.

I don't know how the rest of the pieces will come together, but I am restarting my spiritual journey and ready to fulfill my purpose of sharing and inspiring others to do the same. It has been a true growth in faith and patience. I am not alone, I am not crazy, and I am not scared. I know who I am, I know the way, the light is bright, I found unconditional love, and I am home.

About the Author

Maria Loretto currently still works in private practice, providing individual psychotherapy to clients. She has many plans and projects ahead to help and inspire others and serve her community. She still resides in Connecticut, coparenting her children who are in high school. She feels blessed beyond words and wants nothing but to share that with others.

www.ingramcontent.com/pod-product-compliance
Lightning Source LLC
Chambersburg PA
CBHW031432250726
48656CB00002B/946